Ajijaak yaa enji-mashkegiwang.
Crane is at the marsh.

Doo-miigwanoman maaba
Ajijaak mina-waazowan.
The feathers of the
Crane are a nice color.

Ajijaak

Miigwanag Waabijiiziwag.
The feathers are Gray.

Miigwanag Ozaawiziwag.
The feathers are Brown.

Miigwanag Miskoziwag.
The feathers are Red.

Miigwanag Waabishkiziwag.
The feathers are White.

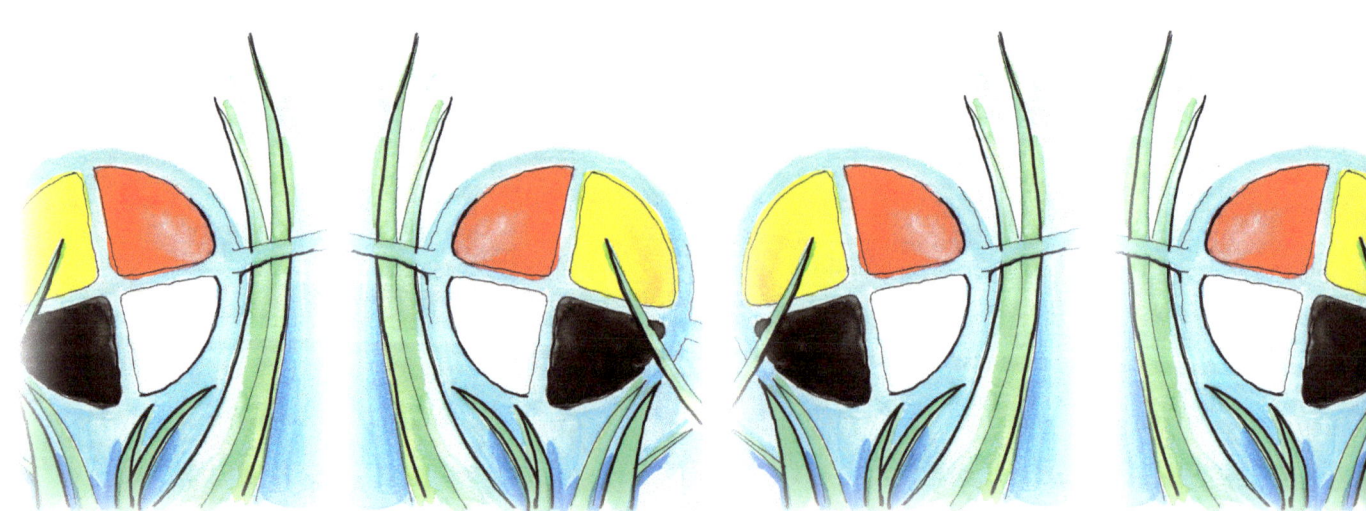

Ajijaak bizindowaan maag'kiin,
Crane listens to the frogs.

Ajijaak waabmaan miskwaadesiinyan.
Crane see's a turtle.

Miskwaadesiinh,
Painted turtle.

Miskwaadesiinh Ozhaawashkozi.
The turtle is Green.

Miskwaadesiinh Ozaawaanzo.
The turtle is Yellow.

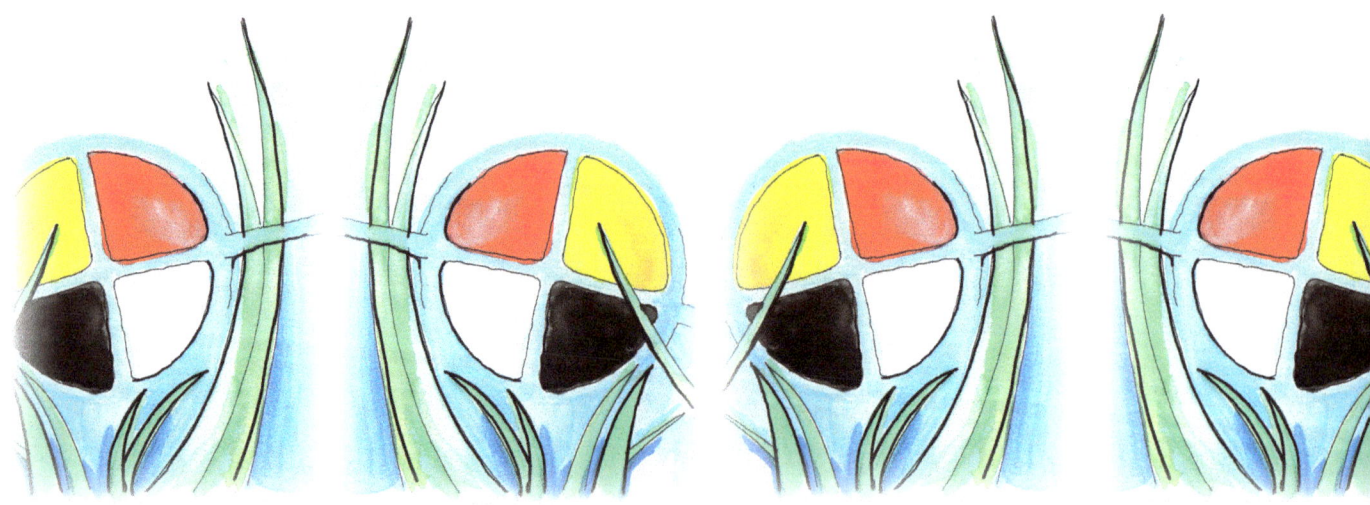

Ajijaak naabi giizhigoong nikeyaa.
Crane looks up towards the sky.

Giizis

Giizis.
The sun.

Waaseyaa-si-ge giizis,
The sun shines.

Biindige-waase-yaa-zhe mitigwaakiing,
Rays of light through the forest.

Mitigoog Ozhaawashkoziwag.
The trees are Green.

Mitigoong

Ajijaak waabi.
Crane see's.

Pitchi,
Robin,

Pitchi Miskozi.
The robin is Red.

Pitchi Ozaawizi.
The robin is Brown.

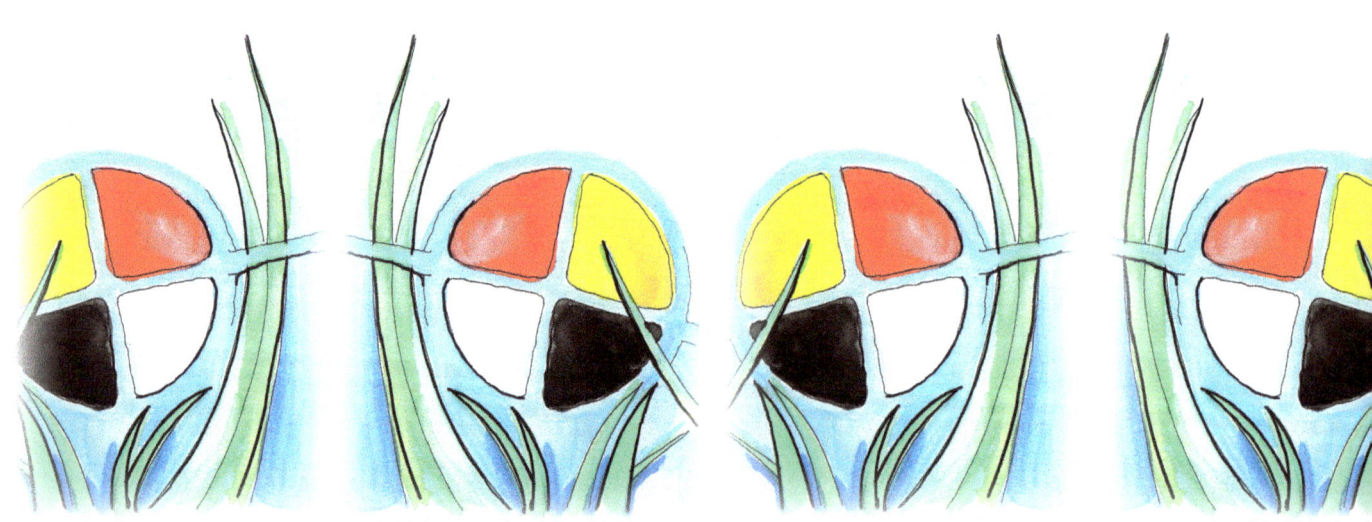

Aandeg,
Crow,

Aaadeg miigwanoman
Makadewiziwag.
Crow's feathers are
Black.

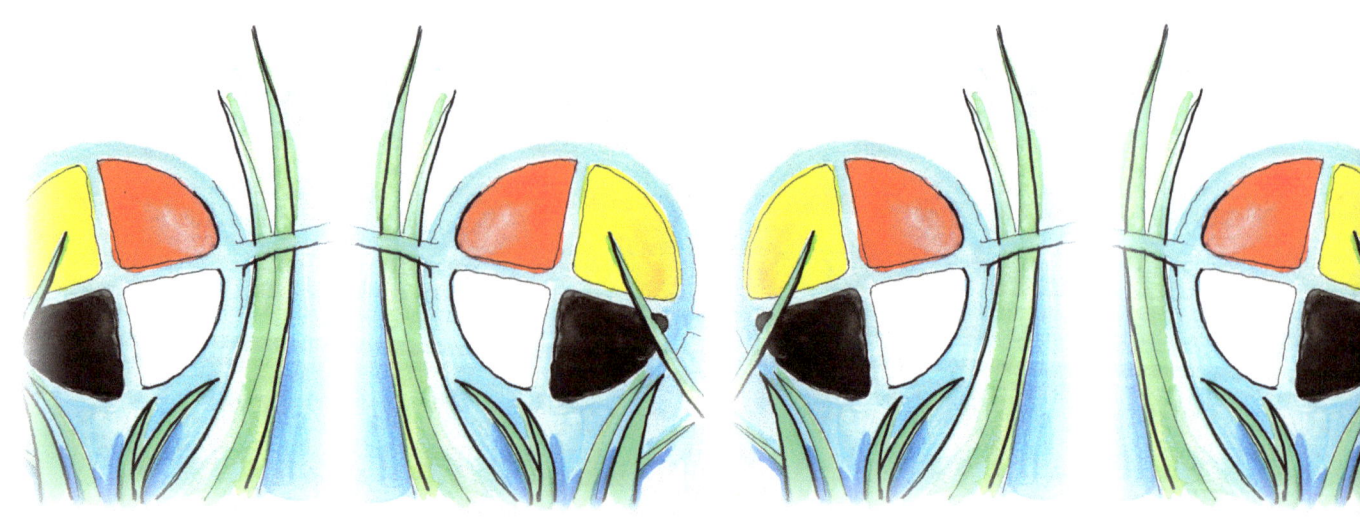

Kina ndamtaawag.
They are busy.

Pitchi mitigoong zhi-gizike,
beshaa Ajijaak yaad.
Robin flies to a tree,
near Crane.

Pitchi ginoonaan Ajijaakwan.
Robin speaks to Crane.

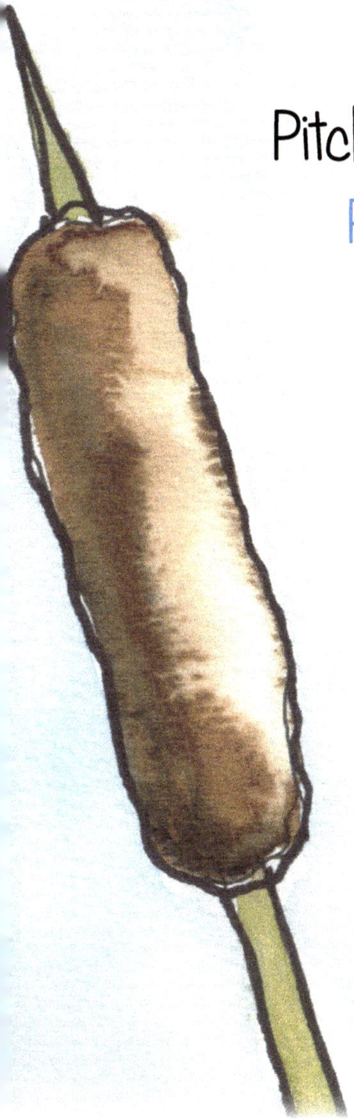

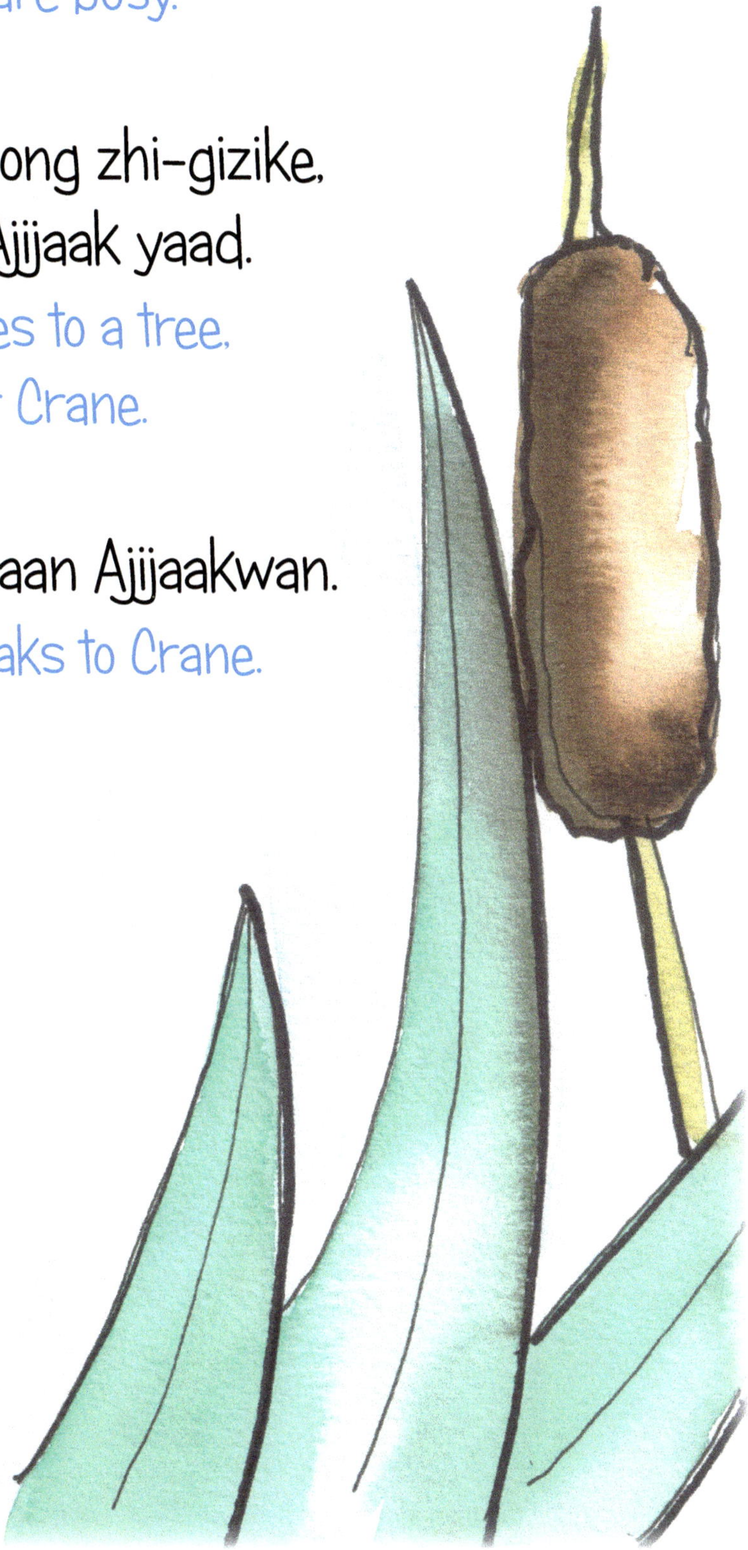

Beshaa enji-mashkegiwang nji-ginoondiwag.
They talk near the marsh.

Ajijaak bizindowaan Pitchiwan.
Crane listens to Robin.

Negaaj bimose Ajijaak.
Crane walks quietly.

Ajijaak zaagtoon enji-maashkegiwang.
Crane loves this marsh.

Ajijaak zhaa tkibiinsing nongo.
Crane travels to the creek today.

Niigaan-nikeyaa miiniwaa ishpiming.
Onward and upward.

Ajijaak bimbazo!
Crane flying!

Ajijaak gizike ishpiming mitigoong,
Crane flies above the tree tops,

Ajijaak waabmaan Migiziin tkibiinsing,
Crane see's Eagle by the creek.

Ajijaak booni gwek shaweying tikibiinsing,
Crane lands right next to the creek,

Migizi miiniwaa Ajijaak ginoondiwag,
Eagle and Crane talk,

Ajijaak bi-maadigaa nbiing.
Crane wades in the water.

Migizi nimadibi mitigoong baashzaamdang nibi.
Eagle sits in a tree over the water.

Migizi miigwanag Ozaawiziwag.
Eagle feathers are Brown.

Migizi shtigwaanim Waabishkaa.
Eagle's head is white.

Migizi giigoonke tkibiinsing.
Eagle catches fish in the creek.

Giigoonyag daawag nbiing.
The fish live in the water.

Miskwaadesiinh daa nbiing.
The turtle lives in the water.

Bineshiinyag nibi minikwewag.
Birds drink water.

Migizi.
Eagle.

Aandeg,
Crow,

Pitchiig,
Robins,

Ajijaak.
Crane.

Ajijaakoog nibi minikwewag.
Cranes drink water.

Nibi aawan bimaadiziwin.
Water is life.

Nibi gchi-twaawan.
Water is sacred.

Ajijaak gchi-piitendaan waabndang noojimoomigak nbiish.

Crane cares to see the water healed.

Ajijaak gnwendaan nibi.

Crane cares for the water.

Naadamooshin naanaagide'endimong nibi.

Help us care for the water.

Migwetch! Mii iw.

Thank you! The End.

FOUR Colours Productions:
www.four-colours.org

Brita Brookes:
Though not of aboriginal descent, Brita has been active in Anishinaabemowin for 10 years. Brita has been taught by Margaret Noodin, Howard Kimewon, Alphonse Pitawanakwat, Ma nee Chacaby, Maya Chacaby, Isadore Toulouse & Shirley Williams. Brita received her Masters Degree from Harvard University & her Bachelor of Science Degree from the University of Michigan. As an Ally, Brita was on the Longest Walk II, participates in ceremony, pow wows, has presented at the A-teg conference 3 times with Albert Owl & Rachel Mae Butzin and at the Manistee Language Camp in Michigan twice with Isadore Toulouse. Brita was a volunteer marketing & moderating the Online Anishinaabemowin program with Isadore Toulouse for 7 years. Brita is a Marketing Specialist & Graphic Designer for a global Architectural & Engineering firm. Her web page is at www.britabrookesgraphics.com

Isadore Toulouse:
Isadore is a speaker and teacher of the Ojibwe and Odawa languages. He is from the community of Wikwemikong Unceded Reserve. For over forty years language has been a priority in Isadore's life. He has worked at various schools, universities and groups teaching language. Isadore has been a critical part of Anishinaabemowin Teg as their President for several terms. This is the 26th year in Sault St. Marie, Michigan for the A-teg language conference. Isadore's book, Kidwenan, published in 1996 is a language resource used across the US and Canada in schools and universities. Isadore shares his skill of language by travelling to conferences and by visiting schools throughout the nation. Thankful to have retained his language he is also thankful to be able to share what he has learned with others and future generations. His stated goal for language is that "it becomes recognized as a first language in the province."

Shirley Ida Williams:

Shirley Ida Williams is a member of the Bird Clan of the Ojibway and Odawa First Nations of Canada. Her Aboriginal name is "Migizi ow-kwe" meaning "that Eagle Woman". She was born and raised at Wikwemikong, First Nations Unceded Reserve on Manitoulin Island. She attended at St. Joseph's Residential School, Spanish, Ontario. Shirley has lectured across Ontario promoting Nishnaabe language and Culture. She received her B.A. degree in Native Studies from Trent University. She received her diploma in Native Language Instructor's Program, Lakehead University and did her M.A. at York University on Environmental Studies on Language and Culture on Manitoulin Dialect in 1996. Shirley started her work in the Native Studies Department in 1986 to develop and promote Native language courses within the department. Shirley is a consultant and sat as an Elder at Sweetgrass First Nation Language Council, for the Woodland Cultural Center, Brantford, Ontario. She has traveled across Ontario to many Native communities and universities giving: lectures, seminars, workshops on various Native issues including language and culture.

www.ingramcontent.com/pod-product-compliance
Lightning Source LLC
Chambersburg PA
CBHW051308110526
44589CB00025B/2971